I0569418

365 DAYS OF
AFFIRMATIONS
Δ Journey of Daily Empowerment

BY AXEL JORDAN

also by axel jordan

sons & shadows
healing (of) hearts
love notes

coming soon,

the journey back
beyond lust

to those on a healing journey,
you are magic
and I am with you.

ΛND SO IT BEGINS ...

Imagine starting each day with a simple yet profound intention—a declaration of who you are, how you feel, and what you seek to create. *365 Days of Affirmations: A Journey of Daily Empowerment* invites you to embrace this practice, nurturing your spirit, aligning your energy, and inspiring personal growth. This is more than a collection of affirmations—it's a journey into mindfulness, healing, and self-discovery.

Each month begins with a week of chakra-focused affirmations, designed to balance your energy centers. You'll start with "I am" for the Root Chakra, grounding yourself in stability and strength. From there, you'll move into "I feel" for the Sacral Chakra, embracing emotions and creativity, and "I do" for the Solar Plexus Chakra, connecting to your inner power and purpose. The journey continues with "I love" for the Heart Chakra, cultivating compassion; "I speak" for the Throat Chakra, honoring your truth; "I see" for the Third Eye Chakra, trusting intuition; and finally, "I understand" for the Crown Chakra, aligning with spiritual harmony.

Beyond the chakra-focused days, daily affirmations for confidence, peace, and purpose guide you through the rest of each month. Paired with mindful activities, these affirmations help you set intentions, create balance, and find joy in everyday moments.

Let *365 Days of Affirmations* be your companion on this path to mindfulness and transformation. One page, one intention, one day at a time—you are about to embark on a journey to your best self.

starting with self-care …

AFFIRMATION:

"I am loved
I am growing
I am healing

I am love
I am growth
I am healed"

MINDFUL ACTIVITY:

Begin this journey with a 3-minute silent meditation.

3-minutes of silent meditation isn't the easiest act of
self-care as during that silence our minds tend to
wander and our body wants to move.
My hope for you is that you begin this journey and
every journey with self-care.

Whether, a 3-minute silent meditation is easy or proves
difficult, I'd like you to continue to work on it.
And, if it's a bit uncomfortable, just remember -
It's when you walk to the edge of the these areas of
discomfort, that you begin to grow the most.

And when you can also do that with kindness towards
yourself, your growth becomes exponential.

DAY 1
Root Chakra

Affirmation

"I am grounded, safe, and secure. I trust the foundation I am building."

Mindful Activity:

Stand with feet shoulder-width apart, visualizing roots extending from your feet into the earth. Feel the energy and strength of the earth travel through those roots and into you. Continue in this exchange for 3 minutes.

DAY 2
Sacral Chakra

Affirmation:

"I feel joy and embrace the richness of my emotions."

Mindful Activity:

Sit quietly five minutes and allow any emotions to surface naturally, observing without judgment. The goal isn't to quiet the thoughts but instead to allow them in peacefully.

DAY 3
Solar Plexus Chakra

Affirmation:

"I do what is necessary to build my dreams with courage and confidence."

Mindful Activity:

Identify a small step toward a personal goal and focus on feeling empowered.

DAY 4
HEART CHAKRA

AFFIRMATION:

"I love myself and accept myself
fully and unconditionally."

MINDFUL ACTIVITY:

Place a hand over your heart, take deep breaths
and repeat the affirmation 6 times.

DAY 5
THROAT CHAKRA

AFFIRMATION:

"I speak my truth openly and authentically."

MINDFUL ACTIVITY:

Write a letter to yourself expressing your thoughts honestly, without judgment.

DAY 6
Third Eye Chakra

Affirmation:

"I see beyond illusions and trust my inner vision."

Mindful Activity:

Close your eyes, visualize a calming indigo light at your forehead, and connect with your intuition.

DAY 7
CROWN CHAKRA

AFFIRMATION:

"I understand my purpose and embrace my connection to the universe.

MINDFUL ACTIVITY:

Reflect on your larger purpose, letting any thoughts come to mind without judgment.

DAY 8

SELF-LOVE AND ACCEPTANCE

AFFIRMATION:

"I honor my feelings and embrace
them without judgment."

MINDFUL ACTIVITY:

Take a few minutes to check in with yourself and
accept any emotions present. Recognizing your
emotions is a powerful tool to also being
able to release what isn't serving you.

DAY 9
GRATITUDE AND APPRECIATION

AFFIRMATION:

"I am grateful for my body and all it does for me."

MINDFUL ACTIVITY:

Take a few moments to gently stretch, honoring the physical body that supports you.

DAY 10

CONFIDENCE AND INNER STRENGTH

AFFIRMATION:

'I am strong, resilient, and capable of handling anything that comes my way."

MINDFUL ACTIVITY:

Reflect on a past challenge and focus on the strength it brought you.

DAY 11
RESILIENCE AND PERSEVERANCE

AFFIRMATION:

"I am resilient and bounce back from any challenge."

MINDFUL ACTIVITY:

Recall a difficult experience and
how it made you stronger.

DAY 12

MINDFULNESS AND PRESENCE

AFFIRMATION:

"I am fully present in this moment."

MINDFUL ACTIVITY:

Take three deep breaths, focusing on the sensation of each inhale and exhale.

DAY 13
MANIFESTATION AND ABUNDANCE

AFFIRMATION:

"I am open to receiving limitless abundance."

MINDFUL ACTIVITY:

Visualize a warm light surrounding you, filling you with abundance.

DAY 14
Forgiveness and Letting Go

Affirmation:

"I forgive myself for past tumbles
and embrace growth."

Mindful Activity:

Write down a past mishap and reflect
on the lessons it taught you.

DAY 15
HEALTH AND WELLNESS

AFFIRMATION:

"I honor my body by giving it the
care and attention it deserves."

MINDFUL ACTIVITY:

Take a few minutes to stretch or gently massage areas
of tension, tuning into your body's needs.

DAY 16

RELATIONSHIPS AND CONNECTION

AFFIRMATION:

"I am grateful for the loving connections in my life."

MINDFUL ACTIVITY:

Write down the names of three people who bring love into your life and send them silent gratitude.

DAY 17
PURPOSE AND MOTIVATION

AFFIRMATION:

"I am motivated to pursue my dreams with courage."

MINDFUL ACTIVITY:

Write down one dream and an action you can take today to move closer to it.

DAY 18

PEACE AND CALM

AFFIRMATION:

"I am at peace with where I am in life."

MINDFUL ACTIVITY:

Take a deep breath and affirm, "I am exactly where need to be," releasing worry or doubt.

DAY 19
CREATIVITY AND INSPIRATION

AFFIRMATION:

"I am a creative being, and my ideas flow effortlessly."

MINDFUL ACTIVITY:

Set a timer for five minutes and free-write anything that comes to mind without judgment.

DAY 20
POSITIVITY AND OPTIMISM

AFFIRMATION:

"I am open to the joy and possibilities each day brings."

MINDFUL ACTIVITY:

Start your day by listing three things you're looking forward to.

DAY 21
HEALING AND SELF-COMPASSION

AFFIRMATION:

"I am gentle with myself as I heal and grow."

MINDFUL ACTIVITY:

Place your hand over your heart and take deep breaths, focusing on sending warmth and compassion inward.

DAY 22

SPIRITUALITY AND CONNECTION

AFFIRMATION:

"I am in harmony with the universe
and trust in its wisdom."

MINDFUL ACTIVITY:

Spend a few moments in stillness, connecting to
your breath and feeling a sense of oneness.

DAY 23
SELF-LOVE AND ACCEPTANCE

AFFIRMATION:

"I am proud of all I have overcome."

MINDFUL ACTIVITY:

Reflect on a past challenge and note the strength you gained from it.

DAY 24

GRATITUDE AND APPRECIATION

AFFIRMATION:

"I am thankful for my mind and the
ability to learn and grow."

MINDFUL ACTIVITY:

Take a moment to read or learn something new,
feeling gratitude for your mind's resilience.

DAY 25
CONFIDENCE AND INNER STRENGTH

AFFIRMATION:

"I believe in my ability to create positive change."

MINDFUL ACTIVITY:

Think of one small way you can make a positive difference today and take action.

DAY 26
Resilience and Perseverance

Affirmation:

"I trust in my ability to adapt and overcome."

Mindful Activity:

Write down a recent change and two
positive outcomes it led to.

DAY 27

MINDFULNESS AND PRESENCE

AFFIRMATION:

"I release distractions and embrace focus."

MINDFUL ACTIVITY:

Set aside five minutes to sit quietly, focusing solely on your breathing.

DAY 28

Mᴀɴɪꜰᴇꜱᴛᴀᴛɪᴏɴ ᴀɴᴅ Aʙᴜɴᴅᴀɴᴄᴇ

Aꜰꜰɪʀᴍᴀᴛɪᴏɴ:

"I am grateful for the abundance I have
and the abundance on its way."

Mɪɴᴅꜰᴜʟ Aᴄᴛɪᴠɪᴛʏ:

List five things you're grateful for, noticing
the abundance that exists in your life.

DAY 29
Forgiveness and Letting Go

Affirmation:

"I forgive others to set myself free."

Mindful Activity:

Write a letter to someone you need to forgive, expressing your feelings, then let them go.

DAY 30
HEALTH AND WELLNESS

AFFIRMATION:

"I am grateful for my body's ability to heal."

MINDFUL ACTIVITY:

Visualize a bright, healing light surrounding any area of your body that needs care, filling it with energy and wellness

DAY 31
ROOT CHAKRA

AFFIRMATION

"I am resilient and adaptable."

MINDFUL ACTIVITY:

Recall a challenge you overcame, focusing on the strength it brought you.

DAY 32
Sacral Chakra

Affirmation:

"I feel connected to my creativity
and let it flow freely."

Mindful Activity:

Spend 10 minutes doing something creative,
like doodling or journaling.

DAY 33
Solar Plexus Chakra

AFFIRMATION

"I do what aligns with my values, knowing I am capable and strong."

MINDFUL ACTIVITY:

List three core values and one way you live by each of them.

DAY 34
HEART CHAKRA

AFFIRMATION:

"I love deeply and bring compassion
into every connection."

MINDFUL ACTIVITY:

Think of someone you care about and visualize
sending them love and kindness.

DAY 35
THROAT CHAKRA

AFFIRMATION

"I speak with confidence and clarity."

MINDFUL ACTIVITY:

Practice saying a positive affirmation aloud, focusing on clarity in your voice.

DAY 36
THIRD EYE CHAKRA

AFFIRMATION:

"I trust my intuition and inner wisdom."

MINDFUL ACTIVITY:

Reflect quietly on a recent decision where you trusted your intuition, appreciating its guidance.

DAY 37
CROWN CHAKRA

AFFIRMATION

"I release all limitations and embrace spiritual growth."

MINDFUL ACTIVITY:

Reflect on what growth means to you, visualizing yourself expanding and evolving spiritually.

DAY 38
SELF-LOVE AND ACCEPTANCE

AFFIRMATION:

"I choose to be kind to myself every day."

MINDFUL ACTIVITY:

Practice self-compassion by saying something kind to yourself each time a self-critical thought arises.

DAY 39

Gratitude and Appreciation

Affirmation

"I am grateful for the simple joys in my life."

Mindful Activity:

Write down three small things that brought you joy today, no matter how small.

DAY 40

CONFIDENCE AND INNER STRENGTH

AFFIRMATION:

"I am confident in my unique path."

MINDFUL ACTIVITY:

Stand in a power pose for 2 minutes, feeling the energy of confidence flowing through you.

DAY 41
RESILIENCE AND PERSEVERANCE

AFFIRMATION

"I am capable of handling whatever comes my way."

MINDFUL ACTIVITY:

Stand tall and take deep breaths, visualizing yourself confidently facing any challenge.

DAY 42
MINDFULNESS AND PRESENCE

AFFIRMATION:

"I let go of the past and future, embracing the now."

MINDFUL ACTIVITY:

Bring your mind back to the present each time it wanders, focusing on one thing you see or hear

DAY 43

Manifestation and Abundance

Affirmation

"I am grateful for my journey and open to new opportunities."

Mindful Activity:

Write down one area of your life where you're open to receiving abundance.

DAY 44
FORGIVENESS AND LETTING GO

AFFIRMATION:

"I release all resentment and choose peace."

MINDFUL ACTIVITY:

Visualize resentment as a dark cloud, and with each breath, imagine it dissolving and leaving space for peace.

DAY 45
HEALTH AND WELLNESS

AFFIRMATION

"I nourish my body with healthy choices."

MINDFUL ACTIVITY:

Choose one nutritious meal or snack, savoring each bite and acknowledging its benefits for your body.

DAY 46

RELATIONSHIPS AND CONNECTION

AFFIRMATION:

"I nurture my relationships with love and respect."

MINDFUL ACTIVITY:

Reach out to a loved one with a kind message or gesture to show appreciation.

DAY 47
Purpose and Motivation

Affirmation

"I am inspired and take steps toward my vision every day."

Mindful Activity:

Visualize yourself achieving a major goal, feeling the excitement and satisfaction it brings.

DAY 48
Peace and Calm

AFFIRMATION:

"I release tension and embrace relaxation."

MINDFUL ACTIVITY:

Do a brief body scan, noticing any areas of tension, and consciously relax each area as you breathe out.

DAY 49
CREATIVITY AND INSPIRATION

AFFIRMATION

"I trust in my creative process and follow it freely."

MINDFUL ACTIVITY:

Work on a creative project without aiming for perfection, simply enjoying the process.

DAY 50
POSITIVITY AND OPTIMISM

AFFIRMATION:

"I believe that everything is working out for my highest good."

MINDFUL ACTIVITY:

Write down a current situation and list three ways it could lead to positive outcomes.

DAY 51
HEALING AND SELF-COMPASSION

AFFIRMATION

"I am grateful for the journey of
healing and self-discovery."

MINDFUL ACTIVITY:

Reflect on one moment of healing and the insight
it provided, feeling gratitude for the journey.

DAY 52

SPIRITUALITY AND CONNECTION

AFFIRMATION:

"I am grateful for my spiritual journey
and the growth it brings."

MINDFUL ACTIVITY:

Reflect on how your spiritual journey has evolved
and appreciate the lessons it has brought.

DAY 53
SELF-LOVE AND ACCEPTANCE

AFFIRMATION

"I am enough, just as I am."

MINDFUL ACTIVITY:

Stand tall, take five deep breaths,
and affirm your worth.

DAY 54

GRATITUDE AND APPRECIATION

AFFIRMATION:

"I appreciate the beauty in the small moments of life."

MINDFUL ACTIVITY:

Observe something simple yet beautiful in your environment, like a plant or the sky.

DAY 55
CONFIDENCE AND INNER STRENGTH

AFFIRMATION

"I am confident in my unique talents and gifts."

MINDFUL ACTIVITY:

Write down three unique qualities or talents you possess and reflect on how they positively impact your life.

DAY 56
Resilience and Perseverance

Affirmation:

"I am patient with myself as I grow stronger."

Mindful Activity:

Reflect on one area of your life where you'd like to build resilience, and note one small step to start.

DAY 57
MINDFULNESS AND PRESENCE

AFFIRMATION

"I am grateful for this moment of life."

MINDFUL ACTIVITY:

Pause and take in a few moments of gratitude for being alive and experiencing the world around you.

DAY 58

MANIFESTATION AND ABUNDANCE

AFFIRMATION:

"I am open to receiving unexpected blessings."

MINDFUL ACTIVITY:

Reflect on past moments where unexpected blessings appeared, reaffirming that good things are always on their way.

DAY 59
FORGIVENESS AND LETTING GO

AFFIRMATION

"I release the need for perfection
and embrace my true self."

MINDFUL ACTIVITY:

Identify one area where you seek perfection and
practice letting go by doing something imperfectly
with acceptance.

DAY 60

HEALTH AND WELLNESS

AFFIRMATION:

"I respect my body's boundaries
and honor its limitations."

MINDFUL ACTIVITY:

Reflect on any activities that may strain you, and
consider one way to adjust or give yourself more rest.

DAY 61
Root Chakra

AFFIRMATION

"I am grounded, safe, and secure."

MINDFUL ACTIVITY:

Stand with feet shoulder-width apart, visualizing roots connecting you to the earth as you breathe deeply.

DAY 62
SACRAL CHAKRA

AFFIRMATION:

"I feel joy and embrace the richness of my emotions."

MINDFUL ACTIVITY:

Engage in a creative activity for a few minutes, allowing yourself to express joy through it

DAY 63
Solar Plexus Chakra

Affirmation

"I do what is necessary to build my dreams with courage and confidence."

Mindful Activity:

Identify a small step toward a personal goal and focus on feeling empowered.

DAY 64
HEART CHAKRA

AFFIRMATION:

"I love myself and accept myself
fully and unconditionally."

MINDFUL ACTIVITY:

Place a hand over your heart, take deep
breaths, and repeat the affirmation.

DAY 65
THROAT CHAKRA

AFFIRMATION

"I speak my truth openly and authentically."

MINDFUL ACTIVITY:

Write a letter to yourself expressing your thoughts honestly, without judgment.

DAY 66
Third Eye Chakra

Affirmation:

"I see beyond illusions and trust my inner vision."

Mindful Activity:

Close your eyes, visualize a calming indigo light at your forehead, and connect with your intuition.

DAY 67
CROWN CHAKRA

AFFIRMATION

"I understand my purpose and embrace my connection to the universe."

MINDFUL ACTIVITY:

Reflect on your larger purpose, letting any thoughts come to mind without judgment.

DAY 68
SELF-LOVE AND ACCEPTANCE

AFFIRMATION:

"I am proud of who I am becoming."

MINDFUL ACTIVITY:

Reflect on one way you've grown recently
and take a moment to celebrate it.

DAY 69
GRATITUDE AND APPRECIATION

AFFIRMATION

"I am grateful for the support I receive from others."

MINDFUL ACTIVITY:

Reach out to a friend or family member to express gratitude for their presence in your life.

DAY 70

CONFIDENCE AND INNER STRENGTH

AFFIRMATION:

"I am resilient and adapt with strength."

MINDFUL ACTIVITY:

Write down three traits you admire in yourself, focusing on how they support your inner strength.

DAY 71
Resilience and Perseverance

Affirmation

"I rise above challenges with courage and resilience."

Mindful Activity:

Recall a time you acted courageously,
letting that memory inspire you today.

DAY 72

MINDFULNESS AND PRESENCE

AFFIRMATION:

"I find joy in the here and now."

MINDFUL ACTIVITY:

Think of something small that brings you joy,
like a favorite song or drink, and take
a few moments to savor it fully.

DAY 73

MANIFESTATION AND ABUNDANCE

AFFIRMATION

"I align my energy with the flow of abundance."

MINDFUL ACTIVITY:

Spend a few minutes breathing deeply, visualizing each inhale bringing in abundance

DAY 74
FORGIVENESS AND LETTING GO

AFFIRMATION:

"I forgive myself and let go of past regrets."

MINDFUL ACTIVITY:

Write a letter of forgiveness to yourself, releasing any lingering guilt or regret.

DAY 75
HEALTH AND WELLNESS

AFFIRMATION

"I am mindful of my body and its needs."

MINDFUL ACTIVITY:

Spend a few moments in deep breathing,
noticing any areas of tension and
releasing them.

DAY 76

Relationships and Connection

Affirmation:

"I am worthy of healthy, loving relationships."

Mindful Activity:

Write down three qualities that make you a valuable friend or partner.

DAY 77
Purpose and Motivation

Affirmation

"I am clear about my goals and
confident in my direction."

Mindful Activity:

Write down your top three goals and one step
you'll take this week to move toward each one.

DAY 78
PEACE AND CALM

AFFIRMATION:

"I create moments of calm in my day."

MINDFUL ACTIVITY:

Take a mindful pause in your day to breathe deeply, even if only for a minute.

DAY 79
CREATIVITY AND INSPIRATION

AFFIRMATION

"I am inspired by my inner world and imagination."

MINDFUL ACTIVITY:

Close your eyes and visualize a place that
feels Inspiring and peaceful, exploring
it in your mind.

DAY 80
POSITIVITY AND OPTIMISM

AFFIRMATION:

"I choose to see the blessings in every situation."

MINDFUL ACTIVITY:

Reflect on one recent event, no matter how challenging, and identify one positive outcome.

DAY 81
Healing and Self-Compassion

Affirmation

"I embrace the freedom that comes with letting go."

Mindful Activity:

Imagine yourself carrying a heavy weight, then picture putting it down, feeling the lightness of release.

DAY 82

SPIRITUALITY AND CONNECTION

AFFIRMATION:

"I am a channel for love, light, and peace."

MINDFUL ACTIVITY:

Visualize yourself radiating love and peace to those around you, letting it flow from within.

DAY 83
Self-Love and Acceptance

AFFIRMATION

"I am deserving of my own love and affection."

MINDFUL ACTIVITY:

Wrap your arms around yourself in a gentle
hug, feeling the warmth and comfort
of self-love.

DAY 84
GRATITUDE AND APPRECIATION

AFFIRMATION:

"I am thankful for my body's ability to heal."

MINDFUL ACTIVITY:

Visualize a bright, healing light surrounding
any area of your body that needs care.

DAY 85

CONFIDENCE AND INNER STRENGTH

AFFIRMATION

"I am aligned with my truth and unshaken by others' opinions."

MINDFUL ACTIVITY:

Reflect on a personal value that is important to you, and feel the confidence that comes from standing firm in it.

DAY 86
RESILIENCE AND PERSEVERANCE

AFFIRMATION:

"I face challenges with courage and
grow stronger each day."

MINDFUL ACTIVITY:

Reflect on a recent challenge and write down
one positive trait it helped you develop.

DAY 87
MINDFULNESS AND PRESENCE

AFFIRMATION

"I am centered, calm, and in harmony with myself."

MINDFUL ACTIVITY:

Sit with your hand on your heart and focus on your heartbeat, feeling centered and calm.

DAY 88

MANIFESTATION AND ABUNDANCE

AFFIRMATION:

"I attract positivity and wealth with ease."

MINDFUL ACTIVITY:

Visualize yourself as a magnet, attracting positive experiences and resources effortlessly.

DAY 89
FORGIVENESS AND LETTING GO

AFFIRMATION

"I release the past and open my
heart to new beginnings."

MINDFUL ACTIVITY:

Write down one thing from your past that you're
ready to let go of, and discard the paper
as a symbol of release.

DAY 90

HEALTH AND WELLNESS

AFFIRMATION:

"I am worthy of a healthy, balanced life."

MINDFUL ACTIVITY:

Write down three healthy habits you can incorporate into your routine and commit to one.

DAY 91
Root Chakra

AFFIRMATION

"I am stable, grounded, and connected to the Earth."

MINDFUL ACTIVITY:

Stand with your feet firmly on the ground, visualizing roots extending from your feet into the Earth, anchoring you.

DAY 92
Sacral Chakra

AFFIRMATION:

"I feel joy and passion flowing freely within me."

MINDFUL ACTIVITY:

Engage in a brief creative activity, such as drawing or writing, to allow your joy and passion to flow.

DAY 93
Solar Plexus Chakra

Affirmation

"I do what aligns with my true self,
with strength and courage."

Mindful Activity:

Write down one action you can take today that
supports your true self and feel the
strength it brings.

DAY 94
Heart Chakra

AFFIRMATION:

"I love openly and allow myself to
give and receive love."

MINDFUL ACTIVITY:

Visualize your heart space filling with warm, green light,
representing love flowing freely within you.

DAY 95
THROAT CHAKRA

AFFIRMATION

"I speak with confidence, clarity, and authenticity."

MINDFUL ACTIVITY:

Practice speaking a positive affirmation aloud, focusing on clarity and confidence in your voice.

DAY 96
Third Eye Chakra

Affirmation:

"I see my path clearly and trust my intuition to guide me."

Mindful Activity:

Reflect on a time you trusted your intuition, and visualize it as a guiding light on your path.

DAY 97
CROWN CHAKRA

AFFIRMATION

"I understand my connection to the universe and embrace its wisdom."

MINDFUL ACTIVITY:

Sit quietly and imagine a bright light above your head, filling you with universal wisdom and clarity.

DAY 98

SELF-LOVE AND ACCEPTANCE

AFFIRMATION:

"I accept myself as I am and embrace my uniqueness."

MINDFUL ACTIVITY:

Reflect on one unique quality you have,
and write down why you appreciate it

DAY 99
GRATITUDE AND APPRECIATION

AFFIRMATION

"I am grateful for my journey
and the lessons I've learned."

MINDFUL ACTIVITY:

Write down one lesson from a recent
experience that has helped you grow.

DAY 100

CONFIDENCE AND INNER STRENGTH

AFFIRMATION:

"I am proud of my achievements
and honor my growth."

MINDFUL ACTIVITY:

List three achievements you're proud of,
big or small, and celebrate them.

DAY 101
Resilience and Perseverance

Affirmation

"I embrace challenges as opportunities
to grow stronger."

Mindful Activity:

Reflect on a recent challenge and identify one
positive outcome or lesson it brought.

DAY 102

MINDFULNESS AND PRESENCE

AFFIRMATION:

"I am fully present and grateful for this moment."

MINDFUL ACTIVITY:

Pause and focus on your breath, noticing the sensations in your body and feeling grateful for this moment.

DAY 103
MANIFESTATION AND ABUNDANCE

AFFIRMATION

"I am open to abundance and
welcome blessings into my life."

MINDFUL ACTIVITY:

Visualize an abundance of positivity, resources,
or love flowing into your life.

DAY 104
Forgiveness and Letting Go

Affirmation:

"I forgive myself and others, releasing
any hurt with compassion."

Mindful Activity:

Write down a hurt you're ready to release, take a deep
breath, and imagine letting it go with each exhale.

DAY 105
HEALTH AND WELLNESS

AFFIRMATION

"I treat my body with respect and care."

MINDFUL ACTIVITY:

Choose a small act of self-care today, like drinking more water or stretching.

DAY 106

RELATIONSHIPS AND CONNECTION

AFFIRMATION:

"I attract loving and supportive relationships."

MINDFUL ACTIVITY:

Reflect on the qualities you value in relationships and imagine surrounding yourself with people who embody them.

DAY 107
Purpose and Motivation

Affirmation

"I am dedicated to my goals and trust my journey."

Mindful Activity:

Write down one goal and one small action you can take this week to move closer to it.

DAY 108
PEACE AND CALM

AFFIRMATION:

"I release stress and welcome calm into my life."

MINDFUL ACTIVITY:

Take five deep breaths, releasing any tension with each exhale and allowing calm to flow in.

DAY 109
CREATIVITY AND INSPIRATION

AFFIRMATION

"I am a channel for endless creativity and inspiration."

MINDFUL ACTIVITY:

Set aside five minutes to doodle, journal, or brainstorm letting your ideas flow without judgment.

DAY 110
POSITIVITY AND OPTIMISM

AFFIRMATION:

"I choose to see the bright side of life."

MINDFUL ACTIVITY:

Reflect on one positive aspect of a recent situation, even if it seemed challenging at first.

DAY 111
HEALING AND SELF-COMPASSION

AFFIRMATION

"I am patient with myself and
honor my healing process."

MINDFUL ACTIVITY:

Place your hand over your heart, take three deep
breaths, and acknowledge your progress in healing.

DAY 112

SPIRITUALITY AND CONNECTION

AFFIRMATION:

"I am connected to the divine within and around me."

MINDFUL ACTIVITY:

Close your eyes, focus on your breath, and imagine connecting with a greater energy surrounding you.

DAY 113
Self-Love and Acceptance

Affirmation

"I am worthy of all the good that life has to offer."

Mindful Activity:

List three things you feel deserving of and reflect on why you're worthy of them.

DAY 114

GRATITUDE AND APPRECIATION

AFFIRMATION:

"I am grateful for each new day
and the possibilities it brings."

MINDFUL ACTIVITY:

As you start your day, take three deep breaths,
feeling gratitude for today's possibilities.

DAY 115

CONFIDENCE AND INNER STRENGTH

AFFIRMATION

"I believe in myself and my ability to succeed."

MINDFUL ACTIVITY:

Write down one goal and visualize yourself achieving it with confidence and joy.

DAY 116

RESILIENCE AND PERSEVERANCE

AFFIRMATION:

"I am strong, and I overcome any obstacle."

MINDFUL ACTIVITY:

Visualize yourself overcoming a challenge, feeling empowered by your strength and resilience.

DAY 117
MINDFULNESS AND PRESENCE

AFFIRMATION

"I am fully engaged in each moment."

MINDFUL ACTIVITY:

Choose one activity today and focus on doing it slowly and mindfully, noticing each detail.

DAY 118
MANIFESTATION AND ABUNDANCE

AFFIRMATION:

"I am deserving of the prosperity I attract."

MINDFUL ACTIVITY:

Visualize an abundance of prosperity and positivity flowing into your life.

DAY 119
Forgiveness and Letting Go

Affirmation

"I let go of what no longer serves me."

Mindful Activity:

Write down one thought or habit you wish to release, and imagine yourself letting it go with each breath.

DAY 120
HEALTH AND WELLNESS

AFFIRMATION:

"I am grateful for my body and
treat it with love and care."

MINDFUL ACTIVITY:

Take a few minutes to gently stretch or move your
body, expressing gratitude for its strength.

DAY 121
Root Chakra

AFFIRMATION

"I am grounded and secure in who I am."

MINDFUL ACTIVITY:

Stand with feet hip-width apart, imagining roots extending from your feet into the earth, grounding you.

DAY 122
Sacral Chakra

Affirmation:

"I feel connected to my emotions
and embrace them fully."

Mindful Activity:

Spend a few minutes journaling or drawing
to express your emotions freely.

DAY 123
Solar Plexus Chakra

Affirmation

"I do what aligns with my highest self with confidence."

Mindful Activity:

Identify a recent accomplishment that brought you confidence, and reflect on what it means to you.

DAY 124
HEART CHAKRA

AFFIRMATION:

"I love myself and others unconditionally."

MINDFUL ACTIVITY:

Place your hand over your heart, take a few deep breaths, and imagine your heart space filling with love.

DAY 125
THROAT CHAKRA

AFFIRMATION

"I speak my truth with kindness and integrity."

MINDFUL ACTIVITY:

Think of one truth you want to express today and practice saying it in a kind, authentic way.

DAY 126
THIRD EYE CHAKRA

AFFIRMATION:

"I see clearly and trust my inner wisdom."

MINDFUL ACTIVITY:

Sit quietly, close your eyes, and focus on your third eye area, allowing your intuition to guide you.

DAY 127
CROWN CHAKRA

AFFIRMATION

"I understand my place in the universe
and trust in its wisdom."

MINDFUL ACTIVITY:

Visualize a soft light above your head, filling you with
clarity and connection to universal wisdom.

DAY 128
SELF-LOVE AND ACCEPTANCE

AFFIRMATION:

"I am worthy of love and acceptance exactly as I am."

MINDFUL ACTIVITY:

Stand in front of a mirror, look into your eyes, and repeat this affirmation with self-compassion.

DAY 129
Gratitude and Appreciation

Affirmation

"I appreciate the beauty in every small moment."

Mindful Activity:

Spend a few minutes observing your surroundings, finding beauty in a simple detail.

DAY 130

Confidence and Inner Strength

Affirmation:

"I believe in my abilities and trust my journey."

Mindful Activity:

Write down three abilities you're proud of, focusing on how they support your goals.

DAY 131
RESILIENCE AND PERSEVERANCE

AFFIRMATION

"I am strong and resilient in the face of any challenge."

MINDFUL ACTIVITY:

Reflect on a time you showed resilience and think about how that strength continues to serve you.

DAY 132
MINDFULNESS AND PRESENCE

AFFIRMATION:

"I am grounded in this moment,
fully aware of the present."

MINDFUL ACTIVITY:

Take three deep breaths, focusing
entirely on each inhale and exhale.

DAY 133
MANIFESTATION AND ABUNDANCE

AFFIRMATION

"I attract abundance by aligning
my energy with positivity."

MINDFUL ACTIVITY:

Visualize yourself attracting positive energy,
resources, and joy into your life.

DAY 134
FORGIVENESS AND LETTING GO

AFFIRMATION:

"I release all blame and choose compassion."

MINDFUL ACTIVITY:

Write down something you're ready to forgive, feeling compassion as you let it go.

DAY 135
HEALTH AND WELLNESS

AFFIRMATION

"I honor my body and mind with healthy choices."

MINDFUL ACTIVITY:

Commit to one healthy choice today, whether
in nutrition, movement, or rest.

DAY 136
RELATIONSHIPS AND CONNECTION

AFFIRMATION:

"I am open to giving and receiving
love in all my relationships."

MINDFUL ACTIVITY:

Reach out to someone you care about with
a small act of kindness or appreciation.

DAY 137
PURPOSE AND MOTIVATION

AFFIRMATION

"I am guided by purpose and take inspired action toward my goals."

MINDFUL ACTIVITY:

Write down one goal and the next action step to move closer to it.

DAY 138
PEACE AND CALM

AFFIRMATION:

"I am calm, centered, and balanced."

MINDFUL ACTIVITY:

Take a moment to close your eyes, breathe deeply, and imagine yourself surrounded by calm energy.

DAY 139
CREATIVITY AND INSPIRATION

AFFIRMATION

"I am a channel for creativity and inspiration."

MINDFUL ACTIVITY:

Set aside time to engage in a creative activity you enjoy, allowing ideas to flow freely.

DAY 140
POSITIVITY AND OPTIMISM

AFFIRMATION:

"I focus on the positive and embrace life's blessings."

MINDFUL ACTIVITY:

List three positive things that happened today
and reflect on how they made you feel.

DAY 141
HEALING AND SELF-COMPASSION

AFFIRMATION

"I am gentle with myself and
honor my healing journey."

MINDFUL ACTIVITY:

Place your hand on your heart, take a deep breath,
and acknowledge your progress in healing.

DAY 142

SPIRITUALITY AND CONNECTION

AFFIRMATION:

"I am connected to a greater energy
that supports and guides me."

MINDFUL ACTIVITY:

Spend a few quiet minutes feeling the energy around
you, sensing the connection to something greater.

DAY 143
SELF-LOVE AND ACCEPTANCE

AFFIRMATION

"I am proud of who I am and honor my journey."

MINDFUL ACTIVITY:

Write down one positive trait or accomplishment you're proud of, and celebrate it.

DAY 144
GRATITUDE AND APPRECIATION

AFFIRMATION:

"I am thankful for the opportunities that come my way."

MINDFUL ACTIVITY:

Reflect on a recent opportunity, big or small, and appreciate the doors it has opened.

DAY 145
CONFIDENCE AND INNER STRENGTH

AFFIRMATION

"I trust myself to overcome challenges and grow."

MINDFUL ACTIVITY:

Visualize yourself facing a challenge confidently, feeling the strength and courage within.

DAY 146
RESILIENCE AND PERSEVERANCE

AFFIRMATION:

"I am capable of achieving my dreams."

MINDFUL ACTIVITY:

Write down one dream and imagine it coming true, feeling motivated to take action toward it.

DAY 147
MINDFULNESS AND PRESENCE

AFFIRMATION

"I am fully engaged in all that I do."

MINDFUL ACTIVITY:

Choose one task today to complete mindfully, focusing on each detail without distractions.

DAY 148
MANIFESTATION AND ABUNDANCE

AFFIRMATION:

"I am open to receiving limitless blessings."

MINDFUL ACTIVITY:

Visualize blessings flowing into your life, allowing yourself to feel grateful for each one.

DAY 149
FORGIVENESS AND LETTING GO

AFFIRMATION

"I release all judgment and embrace compassion."

MINDFUL ACTIVITY:

Reflect on a situation where you judged yourself
or others, and replace it with compassion.

DAY 150
HEALTH AND WELLNESS

AFFIRMATION:

"I respect my body and mind, nurturing them with care."

MINDFUL ACTIVITY:

Spend a few moments checking in with your body's needs, whether it's hydration, movement, or rest.

DAY 151
Root Chakra

AFFIRMATION

"I am safe, secure, and deeply rooted."

MINDFUL ACTIVITY:

Stand barefoot on the ground, visualizing yourself deeply connected to the earth's energy, grounding you.

DAY 152
SACRAL CHAKRA

AFFIRMATION:

"I feel joy and allow my emotions to flow freely."

MINDFUL ACTIVITY:

Take a moment to reflect on a joyful memory, focusing on how it feels in your body and mind.

DAY 153
SOLAR PLEXUS CHAKRA

AFFIRMATION

"I do what aligns with my purpose
and move forward with courage."

MINDFUL ACTIVITY:

Write down one step you can take today to align with
your purpose, focusing on the confidence it brings.

DAY 154
HEART CHAKRA

AFFIRMATION:

"I love and accept myself and others without conditions."

MINDFUL ACTIVITY:

Visualize your heart space expanding with warmth, sending love to yourself and others.

DAY 155
THROAT CHAKRA

AFFIRMATION

"I speak my truth with clarity and compassion."

MINDFUL ACTIVITY:

Reflect on one truth you want to express, practicing saying it with kindness and honesty.

DAY 156
THIRD EYE CHAKRA

AFFIRMATION:

"I see my life's path clearly and trust my inner vision."

MINDFUL ACTIVITY:

Close your eyes, breathe deeply, and imagine a path ahead of you illuminated by your intuition.

DAY 157
CROWN CHAKRA

AFFIRMATION

"I understand and embrace my place in the universe."

MINDFUL ACTIVITY:

Meditate on the thought of universal connection, visualizing a light connecting you to the world around you.

DAY 158
SELF-LOVE AND ACCEPTANCE

AFFIRMATION:

"I am enough, just as I am."

MINDFUL ACTIVITY:

Stand in front of a mirror, make eye contact with yourself, and repeat this affirmation with sincerity.

DAY 159
GRATITUDE AND APPRECIATION

AFFIRMATION

"I am grateful for each experience that shapes me."

MINDFUL ACTIVITY:

Reflect on a recent experience and write down one way it helped you grow.

DAY 160

CONFIDENCE AND INNER STRENGTH

AFFIRMATION:

"I am worthy of success and happiness."

MINDFUL ACTIVITY:

Visualize yourself achieving a goal, feeling the joy and pride of your success.

DAY 161
RESILIENCE AND PERSEVERANCE

AFFIRMATION

"I grow stronger with every challenge."

MINDFUL ACTIVITY:

List three challenges you've overcome, focusing on the strengths they helped you build.

DAY 162
MINDFULNESS AND PRESENCE

AFFIRMATION:

"I release all distractions and find peace in the present."

MINDFUL ACTIVITY:

Spend five minutes in silence, allowing any thoughts to come and go without attachment.

DAY 163
MANIFESTATION AND ABUNDANCE

AFFIRMATION

"I am a magnet for positive energy and success."

MINDFUL ACTIVITY:

Picture yourself surrounded by positivity, attracting success and joy into your life.

DAY 164

FORGIVENESS AND LETTING GO

AFFIRMATION:

"I forgive myself for any past blunders and embrace growth."

MINDFUL ACTIVITY:

Write a short letter of forgiveness to yourself, acknowledging any regrets and letting them go.

DAY 165
HEALTH AND WELLNESS

AFFIRMATION

"I am grateful for my body's strength and resilience."

MINDFUL ACTIVITY:

Take a few minutes to gently stretch, focusing on the strength and flexibility within your body.

DAY 166
RELATIONSHIPS AND CONNECTION

AFFIRMATION:

"I am grateful for the meaningful
connections in my life."

MINDFUL ACTIVITY:

Think of someone who positively impacts your life,
and consider sending them a kind message.

DAY 167
Purpose and Motivation

Affirmation

"I am focused on my goals
and committed to my vision."

Mindful Activity:

Write down one long-term goal and one step
you can take this week to move toward it.

DAY 168
PEACE AND CALM

AFFIRMATION:

"I find peace in the present moment."

MINDFUL ACTIVITY:

Take a deep breath, close your eyes, and allow a sense of calm to wash over you.

DAY 169
CREATIVITY AND INSPIRATION

AFFIRMATION

"I allow my creativity to flow freely."

MINDFUL ACTIVITY:

Set aside a few minutes for a creative activity, allowing yourself to explore new ideas without judgment.

DAY 170
POSITIVITY AND OPTIMISM

AFFIRMATION:

"I am open to the joy and blessings each day brings."

MINDFUL ACTIVITY:

Write down three things you're looking forward to today, no matter how small.

DAY 171
HEALING AND SELF-COMPASSION

AFFIRMATION

"I am gentle with myself and allow healing to happen naturally."

MINDFUL ACTIVITY:

Place your hand over your heart, take a few deep breaths, and embrace a feeling of compassion.

DAY 172
SPIRITUALITY AND CONNECTION

AFFIRMATION:

"I am one with the universe and trust in its guidance."

MINDFUL ACTIVITY:

Spend a few moments meditating on the thought
of universal oneness, breathing deeply
as you feel the connection.

DAY 173
SELF-LOVE AND ACCEPTANCE

AFFIRMATION

"I am proud of my journey and my growth."

MINDFUL ACTIVITY:

Reflect on one area where you've experienced growth and take a moment to appreciate it.

DAY 174

GRATITUDE AND APPRECIATION

AFFIRMATION:

"I am thankful for each new day
and the chance to grow."

MINDFUL ACTIVITY:

At the start of your day, take a few breaths and
set an intention to embrace new experiences.

DAY 175
CONFIDENCE AND INNER STRENGTH

AFFIRMATION

"I am confident in my abilities
and trust in my strength."

MINDFUL ACTIVITY:

Write down one recent accomplishment that made
you feel proud of yourself, no matter how small.

DAY 176
RESILIENCE AND PERSEVERANCE

AFFIRMATION:

"I embrace life's challenges as opportunities to learn."

MINDFUL ACTIVITY:

Think of a challenge you're currently facing
and list one lesson it may bring.

DAY 177
MINDFULNESS AND PRESENCE

AFFIRMATION

"I find peace and gratitude in the here and now."

MINDFUL ACTIVITY:

Spend a few moments observing your surroundings, focusing on a sense of peace in the present.

DAY 178

MANIFESTATION AND ABUNDANCE

AFFIRMATION:

"I welcome abundance in all forms into my life."

MINDFUL ACTIVITY:

Visualize abundance surrounding you and feel grateful for the ways it's manifesting in your life.

DAY 179
Forgiveness and Letting Go

Affirmation

"I release the past and welcome new beginnings."

Mindful Activity:

Write down one thing from your past that you're
ready to let go of, then tear up the paper
as a symbol of release.

DAY 180

HEALTH AND WELLNESS

AFFIRMATION:

"I nurture my body with love and respect."

MINDFUL ACTIVITY:

Take a few moments to nourish your body with a healthy snack or a few sips of water, focusing on its benefits.

DAY 181
Root Chakra

AFFIRMATION

"I am grounded, secure, and supported."

MINDFUL ACTIVITY:

Stand with your feet firmly planted, visualizing energy rising from the earth to ground and support you.

DAY 182
Sacral Chakra

Affirmation:

"I feel alive, passionate, and in
tune with my emotions."

Mindful Activity:

Reflect on one thing that brings you joy and let
yourself feel fully connected to that emotion.

DAY 183
Solar Plexus Chakra

Affirmation

"I do what empowers me and builds my confidence."

Mindful Activity:

Write down one goal that empowers you and identify a small action to take today to move closer to it.

DAY 184
HEART CHAKRA

AFFIRMATION:

"I love openly and give and receive love freely."

MINDFUL ACTIVITY:

Visualize a warm, green light in your heart, allowing it to expand and fill you with love for yourself and others.

DAY 185
THROAT CHAKRA

AFFIRMATION

"I speak clearly and authentically, expressing my truth."

MINDFUL ACTIVITY:

Practice saying an affirmation aloud with clarity, focusing on the power of your voice.

DAY 186
THIRD EYE CHAKRA

AFFIRMATION:

"I see my path with clarity and follow my intuition."

MINDFUL ACTIVITY:

Close your eyes and visualize a peaceful path ahead of you, allowing your intuition to guide you along it.

DAY 187
CROWN CHAKRA

AFFIRMATION

"I understand that I am connected
to a higher purpose."

MINDFUL ACTIVITY:

Meditate on the idea of universal connection, feeling a
sense of purpose and guidance from the universe.

DAY 188
SELF-LOVE AND ACCEPTANCE

AFFIRMATION:

"I accept myself fully and embrace my journey."

MINDFUL ACTIVITY:

Write down one trait or aspect of yourself you appreciate, focusing on the self-acceptance it brings.

DAY 189
GRATITUDE AND APPRECIATION

AFFIRMATION

"I am grateful for the love and support I receive."

MINDFUL ACTIVITY:

Take a moment to think of one person who supports you and send them silent gratitude.

DAY 190

CONFIDENCE AND INNER STRENGTH

AFFIRMATION:

"I am capable and confident in all I do."

MINDFUL ACTIVITY:

Reflect on one recent success, no matter how small, and celebrate it as a reminder of your capabilities.

DAY 191
RESILIENCE AND PERSEVERANCE

AFFIRMATION

"I am resilient, strong, and adaptable."

MINDFUL ACTIVITY:

Think of a recent challenge, and identify one way it helped you grow stronger.

DAY 192
MINDFULNESS AND PRESENCE

AFFIRMATION:

"I release worry and anchor myself in the present."

MINDFUL ACTIVITY:

Focus on your breathing for a few moments, letting go of any worries and feeling present.

DAY 193
MANIFESTATION AND ABUNDANCE

AFFIRMATION

"I attract abundance in all forms."

MINDFUL ACTIVITY:

Visualize positive energy and abundance flowing into your life, surrounding and supporting you.

DAY 194
FORGIVENESS AND LETTING GO

AFFIRMATION:

"I forgive others to free myself from resentment."

MINDFUL ACTIVITY:

Think of one person you're ready to forgive, focusing on the feeling of lightness and freedom it brings.

DAY 195
HEALTH AND WELLNESS

AFFIRMATION

"I listen to my body and honor its needs."

MINDFUL ACTIVITY:

Take a few deep breaths, tuning into any areas of tension or discomfort and giving them gentle attention.

DAY 196
RELATIONSHIPS AND CONNECTION

AFFIRMATION:

"I attract relationships that uplift and inspire me."

MINDFUL ACTIVITY:

Write down three qualities you value in relationships and visualize them manifesting in your connections.

DAY 197
Purpose and Motivation

Affirmation

"I am dedicated to fulfilling my purpose."

Mindful Activity:

Spend a few minutes writing about what purpose
means to you and one step you can take to
live in alignment with it.

DAY 198
PEACE AND CALM

AFFIRMATION:

"I am centered, calm, and at peace with myself."

MINDFUL ACTIVITY:

Sit quietly for a few minutes, focusing on your breath and the feeling of peace within.

DAY 199
CREATIVITY AND INSPIRATION

AFFIRMATION

"I am inspired by the world around me."

MINDFUL ACTIVITY:

Take a short walk or look out a window, noticing details that spark inspiration.

DAY 200
POSITIVITY AND OPTIMISM

AFFIRMATION:

"I am open to the possibilities each day brings."

MINDFUL ACTIVITY:

Begin your day by listing three things you're looking forward to or feeling positive about.

DAY 201
HEALING AND SELF-COMPASSION

AFFIRMATION

"I am gentle with myself as I heal and grow."

MINDFUL ACTIVITY:

Place your hand on your heart, breathe deeply,
and acknowledge the progress you've
made on your healing journey.

DAY 202
SPIRITUALITY AND CONNECTION

AFFIRMATION:

"I am connected to a greater energy
that supports and guides me."

MINDFUL ACTIVITY:

Spend a few minutes meditating, focusing on your
breath, and imagining a supportive energy around you.

DAY 203
SELF-LOVE AND ACCEPTANCE

AFFIRMATION

"I am worthy of kindness and love,
especially from myself."

MINDFUL ACTIVITY:

List three ways you can show yourself kindness
today, and choose one to put into practice.

DAY 204
GRATITUDE AND APPRECIATION

AFFIRMATION:

"I am thankful for the small blessings in my life."

MINDFUL ACTIVITY:

Reflect on three small things you're grateful for and how they enrich your daily experience.

DAY 205
CONFIDENCE AND INNER STRENGTH

AFFIRMATION

"I trust my inner strength to guide me through life."

MINDFUL ACTIVITY:

Recall a past experience where you showed strength, and let that memory inspire you today.

DAY 206
RESILIENCE AND PERSEVERANCE

AFFIRMATION:

"I have the courage to face life's challenges."

MINDFUL ACTIVITY:

Visualize yourself facing a current challenge with courage, feeling your resilience growing with each breath.

DAY 207
Mindfulness and Presence

Affirmation

"I am mindful of the present
moment and embrace it fully."

Mindful Activity:

Pause, take a few deep breaths, and observe
your surroundings with appreciation.

DAY 208
MANIFESTATION AND ABUNDANCE

AFFIRMATION:

"I am worthy of all the abundance life has to offer."

MINDFUL ACTIVITY:

Write down three things you desire, and visualize them as if they've already manifested.

DAY 209
Forgiveness and Letting Go

Affirmation

"I choose to let go of the past and embrace peace."

Mindful Activity:

Reflect on something from the past that you're ready
to release, and imagine yourself feeling lighter
as you let it go.

DAY 210
HEALTH AND WELLNESS

AFFIRMATION:

"I am grateful for my body and treat it with respect."

MINDFUL ACTIVITY:

Take a few minutes to stretch or move your body, appreciating its strength and resilience.

DAY 211
Root Chakra

AFFIRMATION

"I am secure, grounded, and stable."

MINDFUL ACTIVITY:

Stand barefoot if possible, visualizing energy flowing up from the earth to ground and support you.

DAY 212
SACRAL CHAKRA

AFFIRMATION:

"I feel at peace with my emotions
and embrace my creativity."

MINDFUL ACTIVITY:

Engage in a small creative activity, such as drawing
or writing, and allow your emotions to flow freely.

DAY 212
Solar Plexus Chakra

Affirmation

"I do what is needed to honor my personal power."

Mindful Activity:

Identify one goal you'd like to accomplish and visualize yourself moving toward it with confidence.

DAY 214
HEΛRT CHΛKRΛ

AFFIRMATION:

"I love deeply and open my heart to compassion."

MINDFUL ACTIVITY:

Sit quietly, place a hand over your heart, and imagine a warm, green light expanding from your heart space.

DAY 215
THROAT CHAKRA

AFFIRMATION

"I speak with integrity, expressing my truth openly."

MINDFUL ACTIVITY:

Write down a truth or thought you want to express today, and practice saying it with clarity and kindness.

DAY 216
Third Eye Chakra

AFFIRMATION:

"I see my life's purpose clearly and
follow my inner guidance."

MINDFUL ACTIVITY:

Close your eyes and visualize a calm blue light at your
third eye, bringing clarity to your vision and intuition.

DAY 217
Crown Chakra

AFFIRMATION

"I understand my connection to the universe and embrace its wisdom."

MINDFUL ACTIVITY:

Reflect on the idea of interconnectedness, feeling gratitude for the wisdom and guidance from the universe.

DAY 218
SELF-LOVE AND ACCEPTANCE

AFFIRMATION:

"I am proud of who I am and honor my journey."

MINDFUL ACTIVITY:

Reflect on a personal achievement or moment of growth, and take a moment to feel proud of yourself.

DAY 219
Gratitude and Appreciation

Affirmation

"I am grateful for the abundance in my life."

Mindful Activity:

Write down three things you appreciate about your life, focusing on the abundance they bring.

DAY 220

Confidence and Inner Strength

Affirmation:

"I am courageous and stand strong in my beliefs."

Mindful Activity:

List three beliefs or values that are important to you and reflect on how they guide your actions.

DAY 221
RESILIENCE AND PERSEVERANCE

AFFIRMATION

"I rise above obstacles with courage and resilience."

MINDFUL ACTIVITY:

Recall a challenging experience, focusing on
the inner strength you gained from it.

DAY 222
MINDFULNESS AND PRESENCE

AFFIRMATION:

"I am fully present and embrace
each moment as it comes."

MINDFUL ACTIVITY:

Take a few moments to focus on your breath,
feeling each inhale and exhale fully.

DAY 223
MANIFESTATION AND ABUNDANCE

AFFIRMATION

"I attract positivity, abundance, and joy."

MINDFUL ACTIVITY:

Visualize yourself as a magnet, attracting positive energy and joyful experiences into your life.

DAY 224
FORGIVENESS AND LETTING GO

AFFIRMATION:

"I forgive myself and others, freeing
myself from resentment."

MINDFUL ACTIVITY:

Write down any lingering resentment you feel
and imagine letting it go with each breath.

DAY 225
HEALTH AND WELLNESS

AFFIRMATION

"I am committed to nurturing
my body, mind, and soul."

MINDFUL ACTIVITY:

Choose one action today that supports your well
being, whether it's physical activity, meditation, or rest.

DAY 226
RELATIONSHIPS AND CONNECTION

AFFIRMATION:

"I am surrounded by love and kindness."

MINDFUL ACTIVITY:

Think of a loved one and send them silent gratitude, focusing on the positive energy of your connection.

DAY 227
PURPOSE AND MOTIVATION

AFFIRMATION

"I am focused on my goals and
confident in my direction."

MINDFUL ACTIVITY:

Write down one long-term goal and one small
action step you can take toward it this week.

DAY 228
PEACE AND CALM

AFFIRMATION:

"I release all stress and embrace peace."

MINDFUL ACTIVITY:

Take five deep breaths, letting go of tension with each exhale, and allowing peace to enter with each inhale.

DAY 229
CREATIVITY AND INSPIRATION

AFFIRMATION

"I am inspired by my unique talents and ideas."

MINDFUL ACTIVITY:

Spend a few minutes writing, drawing, or brainstorming without judging your ideas—just let them flow.

DAY 230
POSITIVITY AND OPTIMISM

AFFIRMATION:

"I am open to the good things that come my way."

MINDFUL ACTIVITY:

Begin your day by listing three things you're looking forward to, focusing on the positive possibilities.

DAY 231
HEALING AND SELF-COMPASSION

AFFIRMATION

"I am gentle with myself and
honor my healing journey."

MINDFUL ACTIVITY:

Place your hand on your heart, close your eyes, and
take three deep breaths, focusing on self-compassion.

DAY 232
SPIRITUALITY AND CONNECTION

AFFIRMATION:

"I am a part of something greater
and trust in its guidance."

MINDFUL ACTIVITY:

Spend a few quiet minutes meditating on the thought
of being connected to a larger energy, breathing
deeply as you feel the connection

DAY 233
Self-Love and Acceptance

AFFIRMATION

"I am worthy of all the love and kindness in my life."

MINDFUL ACTIVITY:

Write down three things you love about yourself
and take a moment to appreciate each one.

DAY 234
GRATITUDE AND APPRECIATION

AFFIRMATION:

"I am thankful for each lesson life brings."

MINDFUL ACTIVITY:

Reflect on one recent life lesson and consider how it has positively impacted your journey.

DAY 235
CONFIDENCE AND INNER STRENGTH

AFFIRMATION

"I trust my inner strength and the path I'm on."

MINDFUL ACTIVITY:

Visualize yourself confidently overcoming a challenge and feeling stronger on the other side.

DAY 236
RESILIENCE AND PERSEVERANCE

AFFIRMATION:

"I am capable of facing life's challenges with courage."

MINDFUL ACTIVITY:

Think of one area in your life where you can apply resilience and make a commitment to persevere.

DAY 237
MINDFULNESS AND PRESENCE

AFFIRMATION

"I am present and fully engaged with life."

MINDFUL ACTIVITY:

Spend a few minutes noticing your surroundings and feeling gratitude for this moment.

DAY 238

Manifestation and Abundance

AFFIRMATION:

"I am worthy of abundance in all areas of my life."

MINDFUL ACTIVITY:

Write down three areas where you desire abundance and visualize them manifesting.

DAY 239
FORGIVENESS AND LETTING GO

AFFIRMATION

"I let go of what no longer serves me with ease."

MINDFUL ACTIVITY:

Reflect on one thing you're ready to release, feeling lighter and freer as you let it go.

DAY 240
HEALTH AND WELLNESS

AFFIRMATION:

"I nourish my body and mind with love and respect."

MINDFUL ACTIVITY:

Take a few moments to care for your body, whether through stretching, hydration, or a nourishing snack.

DAY 241
ROOT CHAKRA

AFFIRMATION

"I am grounded, stable, and secure."

MINDFUL ACTIVITY:

Stand tall and visualize roots extending from your feet, anchoring you securely to the earth.

DAY 242
Sᴀᴄʀᴀʟ Cʜᴀᴋʀᴀ

Affirmation:

"I feel joy, creativity, and a connection
to my emotions."

Mindful Activity:

Take a few minutes to express yourself creatively,
whether through drawing, writing, or dancing.

DAY 243
SOLAR PLEXUS CHAKRA

AFFIRMATION

"I do what empowers me and take confident action."

MINDFUL ACTIVITY:

Write down one action that makes you feel
empowered and take a small step toward it.

DAY 244
Heart Chakra

Affirmation:

"I love freely, embracing compassion and kindness."

Mindful Activity:

Place your hand over your heart and imagine a soft
green light radiating love and compassion.

DAY 245
THROAT CHAKRA

AFFIRMATION

"I speak my truth with kindness and confidence."

MINDFUL ACTIVITY:

Think of one thought or feeling you'd like to express, practicing speaking it with clarity and respect.

DAY 246
Third Eye Chakra

Affirmation:

"I see clearly, trusting in my inner guidance."

Mindful Activity:

Close your eyes and visualize a calm blue light at your third eye, focusing on inner clarity.

DAY 247
CROWN CHAKRA

AFFIRMATION

"I understand my place in the universe
and am open to its wisdom."

MINDFUL ACTIVITY:

Meditate on the idea of connection to a higher energy,
feeling the sense of peace it brings.

DAY 248
SELF-LOVE AND ACCEPTANCE

AFFIRMATION:

"I am worthy of love, respect, and kindness."

MINDFUL ACTIVITY:

Reflect on one thing you love about yourself, allowing yourself to feel genuine appreciation.

DAY 249
GRATITUDE AND APPRECIATION

AFFIRMATION

"I am grateful for the beauty that surrounds me."

MINDFUL ACTIVITY:

Spend a few moments observing something beautiful, like nature or art, and feel gratitude for it.

DAY 250
CONFIDENCE AND INNER STRENGTH

AFFIRMATION:

"I believe in my abilities and am proud of who I am."

MINDFUL ACTIVITY:

Write down three accomplishments you're proud of,
reflecting on the confidence they bring.

DAY 251
RESILIENCE AND PERSEVERANCE

AFFIRMATION

"I embrace life's challenges with courage and resilience."

MINDFUL ACTIVITY:

Think of a recent challenge and identify one positive outcome it led to.

DAY 252

MINDFULNESS AND PRESENCE

AFFIRMATION:

"I am fully present and enjoy each
moment as it unfolds."

MINDFUL ACTIVITY:

Spend a few moments focusing on your breath,
feeling each inhale and exhale with awareness.

DAY 253
MANIFESTATION AND ABUNDANCE

AFFIRMATION

"I am open to receiving abundance
in all areas of my life."

MINDFUL ACTIVITY:

Visualize yourself surrounded by abundance, feeling
gratitude for the positive energy it brings.

DAY 254
Forgiveness and Letting Go

Affirmation:

"I forgive myself and release any guilt or regret."

Mindful Activity:

Write down any lingering regrets and imagine letting them go with each breath.

DAY 255
HEALTH AND WELLNESS

AFFIRMATION

"I honor my body by taking care of its needs."

MINDFUL ACTIVITY:

Choose one healthy choice today, such as drinking water, stretching, or getting enough rest.

DAY 256

RELATIONSHIPS AND CONNECTION

AFFIRMATION:

"I am grateful for the supportive
relationships in my life."

MINDFUL ACTIVITY:

Reach out to someone you appreciate
and share a kind message with them.

DAY 257
PURPOSE AND MOTIVATION

AFFIRMATION

"I am dedicated to fulfilling my goals with passion and persistence."

MINDFUL ACTIVITY:

Write down one goal and list three reasons why it's meaningful to you.

DAY 258
Peace and Calm

Affirmation:

"I am at peace with myself and the world around me."

Mindful Activity:

Take a deep breath, close your eyes, and let go of any tension, focusing on inner peace.

DAY 259
CREATIVITY AND INSPIRATION

AFFIRMATION

"I allow my creativity to flow without limitation."

MINDFUL ACTIVITY:

Set aside five minutes to doodle, brainstorm, or write freely, letting ideas come naturally.

DAY 260
Positivity and Optimism

Affirmation:

"I am open to the blessings life has to offer."

Mindful Activity:

Begin your day by listing three things you're looking forward to or feeling positive about.

DAY 261
Healing and Self-Compassion

Affirmation

"I am gentle with myself, embracing each step of my healing journey."

Mindful Activity:

Place your hand on your heart, take a few deep breaths, and acknowledge any progress in healing.

DAY 262
Spirituality and Connection

Affirmation:

"I am connected to a loving, supportive energy around me."

Mindful Activity:

Spend a few moments in quiet meditation, feeling connected to a universal energy of love.

DAY 263
Self-Love and Acceptance

AFFIRMATION

"I am proud of my progress and my personal growth."

MINDFUL ACTIVITY:

Write down one area where you've experienced growth and take a moment to appreciate it.

DAY 264
GRATITUDE AND APPRECIATION

AFFIRMATION:

"I am thankful for the positive influences in my life."

MINDFUL ACTIVITY:

Reflect on one person or experience that has positively shaped you, and send silent gratitude for it.

DAY 265
Confidence and Inner Strength

Affirmation

"I trust my inner strength to guide me forward."

Mindful Activity:

Visualize yourself confidently facing a challenge, feeling grounded in your inner strength.

DAY 266

RESILIENCE AND PERSEVERANCE

AFFIRMATION:

"I have the courage to persevere
and achieve my goals."

MINDFUL ACTIVITY:

Write down one challenge you're currently facing,
reminding yourself of your ability to overcome it.

DAY 267
MINDFULNESS AND PRESENCE

AFFIRMATION

"I embrace each moment with
full awareness and gratitude."

MINDFUL ACTIVITY:

Take a short walk or sit quietly, observing your
surroundings with gratitude for the present.

DAY 268

MANIFESTATION AND ABUNDANCE

AFFIRMATION:

"I am open to the flow of abundance in my life."

MINDFUL ACTIVITY:

Write down three areas in which you would like to experience abundance and visualize them unfolding.

DAY 269
FORGIVENESS AND LETTING GO

AFFIRMATION

"I release past hurts and make
space for peace and love."

MINDFUL ACTIVITY:

Reflect on a past hurt you're ready to let go of,
imagining it dissolving with each exhale.

DAY 270
Health and Wellness

Affirmation:

"I nurture my body with mindful choices."

Mindful Activity:

Choose a nutritious snack or meal today, savoring each bite and appreciating its nourishment.

DAY 271
Root Chakra

AFFIRMATION

"I am grounded, centered, and at peace."

MINDFUL ACTIVITY:

Stand with both feet firmly on the ground, visualizing stability and grounding energy flowing up from the earth.

DAY 272
Sacral Chakra

AFFIRMATION:

"I feel joy, creativity, and a deep
connection to my inner self."

MINDFUL ACTIVITY:

Spend a few moments engaging in a creative activity
that brings you joy, such as journaling or drawing.

DAY 273
Solar Plexus Chakra

Affirmation

"I do what is right for me with confidence and strength."

Mindful Activity:

Write down one decision you made recently that empowered you and reflect on the strength it brought.

DAY 274
Heart Chakra

Affirmation:

"I love openly and allow myself to
give and receive love freely."

Mindful Activity:

Place your hand over your heart and visualize a warm,
green light radiating love and compassion.

DAY 275
Throat Chakra

Affirmation

"I speak my truth clearly and respectfully."

Mindful Activity:

Think of one thing you'd like to communicate today and practice saying it with honesty and kindness.

DAY 276
THIRD EYE CHAKRA

AFFIRMATION:

"I see my inner truth and trust my intuition."

MINDFUL ACTIVITY:

Close your eyes and focus on the space between
your eyebrows, letting your mind clear
as you tune into your intuition.

DAY 277
CROWN CHAKRA

AFFIRMATION

"I understand and embrace my connection to the universe."

MINDFUL ACTIVITY:

Meditate quietly on the feeling of oneness with all things, visualizing a light connecting you to the universe.

DAY 278
SELF-LOVE AND ACCEPTANCE

AFFIRMATION:

"I am worthy of love and compassion."

MINDFUL ACTIVITY:

Look into the mirror and say this affirmation aloud, focusing on accepting yourself fully.

DAY 279
GRATITUDE AND APPRECIATION

AFFIRMATION

"I am grateful for each blessing, big and small."

MINDFUL ACTIVITY:

Write down three small things you're grateful for and take a moment to appreciate each one.

DAY 280
CONFIDENCE AND INNER STRENGTH

AFFIRMATION:

"I am confident and trust in my abilities."

MINDFUL ACTIVITY:

Recall a recent success and reflect on the confidence it brought you, no matter how small.

DAY 281
RESILIENCE AND PERSEVERANCE

AFFIRMATION

"I am resilient and able to overcome any obstacle."

MINDFUL ACTIVITY:

Think of a challenge you've faced in the past, and remember how it strengthened your resilience.

DAY 282
MINDFULNESS AND PRESENCE

AFFIRMATION:

"I embrace the present moment and let go of worry."

MINDFUL ACTIVITY:

Take a few moments to focus on your breath,
releasing any worries with each exhale.

DAY 283
Manifestation and Abundance

Affirmation

"I am open to the abundance flowing into my life."

Mindful Activity:

Visualize positive energy and abundance surrounding you, filling every aspect of your life.

DAY 284
FORGIVENESS AND LETTING GO

AFFIRMATION:

"I release all resentment and choose to forgive."

MINDFUL ACTIVITY:

Write down any resentments you feel ready to release and visualize letting go with each breath.

DAY 285
HEALTH AND WELLNESS

AFFIRMATION

"I care for my body, mind, and
spirit with love and respect."

MINDFUL ACTIVITY:

Take a moment to listen to your body's needs, whether
it's rest, movement, or hydration, and honor that need.

DAY 286
Relationships and Connection

Affirmation:

"I am grateful for the love and support in my life."

Mindful Activity:

Reflect on one person who brings love and support to your life, and send them silent gratitude.

DAY 287
Purpose and Motivation

Affirmation

"I am dedicated to my goals and follow my purpose."

Mindful Activity:

Write down a goal that aligns with your purpose, focusing on the motivation it brings.

DAY 288
Peace and Calm

AFFIRMATION:

"I am at peace with where I am in life."

MINDFUL ACTIVITY:

Close your eyes, take three deep breaths, and visualize peace and calm filling every part of your body.

DAY 289
Creativity and Inspiration

Affirmation

"I am inspired by the beauty and wonder around me.

Mindful Activity:

Spend a few minutes observing something beautiful in your surroundings and allow it to spark inspiration.

DAY 290

Positivity and Optimism

Affirmation:

"I am open to the positive opportunities each day brings."

Mindful Activity:

Start your day by listing three things you're looking forward to, focusing on the positive energy it brings.

DAY 291
HEALING AND SELF-COMPASSION

AFFIRMATION

"I am patient with myself as I heal and grow."

MINDFUL ACTIVITY:

Place your hand over your heart, take three deep breaths, and feel a sense of compassion for your healing journey.

DAY 292

SPIRITUALITY AND CONNECTION

AFFIRMATION:

"I am connected to a higher power
that supports and guides me."

MINDFUL ACTIVITY:

Meditate on the idea of a higher power supporting
you, feeling comforted by the guidance it offers.

DAY 293
SELF-LOVE AND ACCEPTANCE

AFFIRMATION

"I am proud of the person I am becoming."

MINDFUL ACTIVITY:

Reflect on one positive change you've made recently, celebrating your progress and growth.

DAY 294
GRATITUDE AND APPRECIATION

AFFIRMATION:

"I am thankful for every experience
that helps me grow."

MINDFUL ACTIVITY:

Write down one recent experience that helped you
grow, appreciating the lessons it brought.

DAY 295
CONFIDENCE AND INNER STRENGTH

AFFIRMATION

"I believe in my strength and ability
to achieve my dreams."

MINDFUL ACTIVITY:

Visualize yourself achieving a goal, feeling
proud and confident in your abilities.

DAY 296
RESILIENCE AND PERSEVERANCE

AFFIRMATION:

"I have the courage and resilience
to face any challenge."

MINDFUL ACTIVITY:

Think of a current challenge, imagining yourself
facing it with strength and determination.

DAY 297
MINDFULNESS AND PRESENCE

AFFIRMATION

"I am fully present and engaged in each moment."

MINDFUL ACTIVITY:

Spend a few moments observing your surroundings, focusing on being fully present.

DAY 298

MANIFESTATION AND ABUNDANCE

AFFIRMATION:

"I welcome abundance into my life with gratitude."

MINDFUL ACTIVITY:

Write down three things you desire, feeling gratitude as if they've already come into your life.

DAY 299
FORGIVENESS AND LETTING GO

AFFIRMATION

"I let go of past hurts and make
room for peace and love."

MINDFUL ACTIVITY:

Visualize a past hurt you're ready to release,
breathing out as you let it go.

DAY 300
HEALTH AND WELLNESS

AFFIRMATION:

"I respect my body and treat it with care and love."

MINDFUL ACTIVITY:

Choose a small act of self-care today, such as drinking water, taking a short walk, or stretching.

DAY 301
Root Chakra

AFFIRMATION

"I am stable, secure, and grounded in the present."

MINDFUL ACTIVITY:

Stand with feet shoulder-width apart, feeling the earth's stability beneath you, and visualize a grounding energy flowing upward.

DAY 302
Sacral Chakra

Affirmation:

"I feel joy and embrace my emotions with ease."

Mindful Activity:

Reflect on a joyful memory or activity and let yourself reconnect with that feeling, noticing how it feels in your body.

DAY 303
Solar Plexus Chakra

Affirmation

"I do what aligns with my true
self and feel empowered."

Mindful Activity:

Write down one thing you accomplished recently
that made you feel strong and empowered.

DAY 304
HEART CHAKRA

AFFIRMATION:

"I love and accept myself and others fully."

MINDFUL ACTIVITY:

Place your hand over your heart, taking deep breaths, and imagine filling your heart with love and acceptance.

DAY 305
THROAT CHAKRA

AFFIRMATION

"I speak my truth with clarity and kindness."

MINDFUL ACTIVITY:

Practice saying a positive affirmation aloud, focusing on expressing it with clarity and warmth.

DAY 306
THIRD EYE CHAKRA

AFFIRMATION:

"I see the bigger picture and trust my inner wisdom."

MINDFUL ACTIVITY:

Close your eyes and focus on the space between your eyebrows, visualizing a deep indigo light and tuning into your intuition.

DAY 307
CROWN CHAKRA

AFFIRMATION

"I understand my connection to all things
and embrace universal wisdom."

MINDFUL ACTIVITY:

Meditate on the feeling of interconnectedness,
visualizing a light connecting you to the universe.

DAY 308
SELF-LOVE AND ACCEPTANCE

AFFIRMATION:

"I am enough, just as I am."

MINDFUL ACTIVITY:

Stand in front of a mirror, make eye contact with yourself, and repeat this affirmation with love and acceptance.

DAY 309
GRATITUDE AND APPRECIATION

AFFIRMATION

"I am grateful for the love and support I receive."

MINDFUL ACTIVITY:

Write down the names of three people who bring positivity into your life and send them silent gratitude.

DAY 310

CONFIDENCE AND INNER STRENGTH

AFFIRMATION:

"I believe in my strength and my journey."

MINDFUL ACTIVITY:

Think of a recent moment where you showed resilience, and celebrate that strength within you.

DAY 311
RESILIENCE AND PERSEVERANCE

AFFIRMATION

"I am capable of overcoming any
challenge with courage."

MINDFUL ACTIVITY:

Reflect on a time you faced adversity and think
about how it strengthened your resilience.

DAY 312

MINDFULNESS AND PRESENCE

AFFIRMATION:

"I let go of distractions and embrace the present moment."

MINDFUL ACTIVITY:

Spend a few minutes focusing on your breath, letting go of any distractions with each exhale.

DAY 313
MANIFESTATION AND ABUNDANCE

AFFIRMATION

"I attract positivity, abundance, and joy into my life."

MINDFUL ACTIVITY:

Visualize positive energy flowing into your life, filling each area with abundance and happiness.

DAY 314
FORGIVENESS AND LETTING GO

AFFIRMATION:

"I forgive myself and others, freeing myself from the past."

MINDFUL ACTIVITY:

Write down any feelings of regret or resentment and imagine releasing them with each breath.

DAY 315
HEALTH AND WELLNESS

AFFIRMATION

"I care for my body and mind with love and respect."

MINDFUL ACTIVITY:

Take a few moments to check in with your body's needs, whether it's stretching, resting, or nourishing.

DAY 316
Relationships and Connection

Affirmation:

"I am grateful for the meaningful
connections in my life."

Mindful Activity:

Think of one person who brings positivity to
your life and consider reaching out
to express your appreciation.

DAY 317
PURPOSE AND MOTIVATION

AFFIRMATION

"I am focused on my goals and motivated by my purpose."

MINDFUL ACTIVITY:

Write down one goal that aligns with your purpose and list one action you'll take toward it this week.

DAY 318
PEACE AND CALM

AFFIRMATION:

"I am at peace with myself and
with the world around me."

MINDFUL ACTIVITY:

Close your eyes, take a few deep breaths, and
imagine peace filling every part of your body.

DAY 319
CREATIVITY AND INSPIRATION

AFFIRMATION

"I am open to new ideas and inspired
by the world around me."

MINDFUL ACTIVITY:

Take a short walk, observing your surroundings, and let
inspiration flow from the things you see.

DAY 320
Positivity and Optimism

Affirmation:

"I focus on the good things in my
life and welcome positivity."

Mindful Activity:

Begin your day by listing three things you're
looking forward to or feeling positive about.

DAY 321
HEALING AND SELF-COMPASSION

AFFIRMATION

"I am gentle with myself and
honor my healing journey."

MINDFUL ACTIVITY:

Place your hand over your heart, take deep breaths,
and acknowledge your progress in healing.

DAY 322
Spirituality and Connection

Affirmation:

"I am connected to a supportive, guiding energy."

Mindful Activity:

Spend a few quiet moments meditating on the thought of a loving energy surrounding and guiding you.

DAY 323
Self-Love and Acceptance

AFFIRMATION

"I am proud of who I am and who I am becoming."

MINDFUL ACTIVITY:

Reflect on a recent accomplishment, big or small, and feel proud of the steps you're taking.

DAY 324

GRATITUDE AND APPRECIATION

AFFIRMATION:

"I am grateful for the lessons and growth in my life."

MINDFUL ACTIVITY:

Write down one lesson from a recent experience
and consider the growth it has brought.

DAY 325
CONFIDENCE AND INNER STRENGTH

AFFIRMATION

"I trust in my abilities and the path I'm on."

MINDFUL ACTIVITY:

Visualize yourself confidently moving forward on your path, feeling empowered by your strength.

DAY 326
RESILIENCE AND PERSEVERANCE

AFFIRMATION:

"I am strong enough to face any
challenge that comes my way."

MINDFUL ACTIVITY:

Write down one current challenge and list two
strengths that will help you overcome it.

DAY 327
Mindfulness and Presence

Affirmation

"I am fully present and engaged in each moment."

Mindful Activity:

Take a few minutes to tune into your surroundings, fully engaging your senses.

DAY 328

MANIFESTATION AND ABUNDANCE

AFFIRMATION:

"I am worthy of the abundance I desire."

MINDFUL ACTIVITY:

Write down three things you'd like to attract into your life, visualizing each as if it has already manifested.

DAY 329
Forgiveness and Letting Go

Affirmation

"I release the past and open
myself to peace and love."

Mindful Activity:

Reflect on one thing from the past that you're ready
to let go of, breathing out as you release it.

DAY 330
HEALTH AND WELLNESS

AFFIRMATION:

"I nourish my body and mind with care and love."

MINDFUL ACTIVITY:

Choose one healthy habit to incorporate today,
such as drinking water, taking a walk,
or practicing mindful eating.

DAY 331
Root Chakra

AFFIRMATION

"I am strong, grounded, and secure."

MINDFUL ACTIVITY:

Stand with both feet on the ground, feeling stability beneath you, and visualize roots growing from your feet into the earth.

DAY 332
Sacral Chakra

Affirmation:

"I feel joy, passion, and a connection to my emotions."

Mindful Activity:

Spend a few moments engaging in a creative activity that brings you joy, such as drawing or journaling.

DAY 333
SOLAR PLEXUS CHAKRA

AFFIRMATION

"I do what aligns with my purpose and empowers me."

MINDFUL ACTIVITY:

Identify one action that makes you feel empowered, and take a small step toward it today.

DAY 334
HEART CHAKRA

AFFIRMATION:

"I love myself and others without condition."

MINDFUL ACTIVITY:

Place your hand over your heart, breathe deeply, and imagine filling your heart with love and compassion.

DAY 335
THROAT CHAKRA

AFFIRMATION

"I speak my truth with confidence and respect."

MINDFUL ACTIVITY:

Reflect on one truth you want to express, and practice saying it with kindness and clarity.

DAY 336
THIRD EYE CHAKRA

AFFIRMATION:

"I see my path clearly and trust my intuition."

MINDFUL ACTIVITY:

Close your eyes and focus on the space between
your eyebrows, visualizing a soft, calm
light that brings clarity and insight.

DAY 337
CROWN CHAKRA

AFFIRMATION

"I understand my connection to the universe and embrace its wisdom."

MINDFUL ACTIVITY:

Meditate quietly on the feeling of interconnectedness, visualizing a light connecting you to the greater universe.

DAY 338
SELF-LOVE AND ACCEPTANCE

AFFIRMATION:

"I am proud of who I am becoming
and honor my journey."

MINDFUL ACTIVITY:

Reflect on one positive change you've made
recently and take a moment to appreciate it.

DAY 339
GRATITUDE AND APPRECIATION

AFFIRMATION

"I am grateful for the love, support,
and abundance in my life."

MINDFUL ACTIVITY:

Write down three things you're grateful for, focusing
on the abundance they bring to your life.

DAY 340

Confidence and Inner Strength

Affirmation:

"I trust in my abilities and believe in my strength."

Mindful Activity:

Recall a recent success, no matter how small,
and celebrate the confidence it brings.

DAY 341
Resilience and Perseverance

Affirmation

"I am capable of overcoming
any obstacle with courage."

Mindful Activity:

Reflect on a past challenge you overcame, and
acknowledge the resilience it has brought you.

DAY 342
MINDFULNESS AND PRESENCE

AFFIRMATION:

"I am fully present in this moment, free from worry."

MINDFUL ACTIVITY:

Take a few deep breaths, focusing on releasing any thoughts of the past or future.

DAY 343
MANIFESTATION AND ABUNDANCE

AFFIRMATION

"I welcome abundance in all forms into my life."

MINDFUL ACTIVITY:

Visualize abundance flowing into your life, feeling grateful for all that you are attracting.

DAY 344
Forgiveness and Letting Go

Affirmation:

"I forgive myself and others, choosing
peace over resentment."

Mindful Activity:

Write down any lingering resentments you feel
and imagine releasing them with each breath.

DAY 345
HEALTH AND WELLNESS

AFFIRMATION

"I honor my body by caring
for it with love and respect."

MINDFUL ACTIVITY:

Check in with your body's needs today—whether it's
rest, movement, or nourishment—and honor it.

DAY 346

RELATIONSHIPS AND CONNECTION

AFFIRMATION:

"I am surrounded by love and attract
supportive relationships."

MINDFUL ACTIVITY:

Think of someone who brings positivity into your life
and take a moment to send them silent gratitude.

DAY 347
PURPOSE AND MOTIVATION

AFFIRMATION

"I am focused on my goals and
motivated by my dreams."

MINDFUL ACTIVITY:

Write down one goal that excites you, and identify
a small action you can take toward it this week.

DAY 348
PEACE AND CALM

AFFIRMATION:

"I am at peace with who I am and where I am in life."

MINDFUL ACTIVITY:

Close your eyes, take a deep breath, and let go
of any tension, feeling peace filling your body.

DAY 349
CREATIVITY AND INSPIRATION

AFFIRMATION

"I am open to new ideas and inspired
by the world around me."

MINDFUL ACTIVITY:

Take a few minutes to brainstorm or journal freely,
letting your creativity flow without limits.

DAY 350
POSITIVITY AND OPTIMISM

AFFIRMATION:

"I focus on the positive and welcome joy into my life."

MINDFUL ACTIVITY:

Begin your day by listing three things you're looking forward to or feel positive about.

DAY 351
Healing and Self-Compassion

AFFIRMATION

"I am gentle with myself, honoring my journey of healing."

MINDFUL ACTIVITY:

Place your hand on your heart, breathe deeply, and acknowledge any progress you've made.

DAY 352
Spirituality and Connection

Affirmation:

"I am part of a greater whole and trust in its guidance."

Mindful Activity:

Spend a few quiet minutes reflecting on the sense of connection to a higher energy or purpose.

DAY 353
SELF-LOVE AND ACCEPTANCE

AFFIRMATION

"I am deserving of love, kindness,
and respect from myself."

MINDFUL ACTIVITY:

List three things you love about yourself, and
take a moment to celebrate each one.

DAY 354
GRATITUDE AND APPRECIATION

AFFIRMATION:

"I am grateful for each experience
that helps me grow."

MINDFUL ACTIVITY:

Reflect on one recent experience that brought
growth and appreciate the lessons it offered.

DAY 355
CONFIDENCE AND INNER STRENGTH

AFFIRMATION

"I trust my inner strength and embrace my journey."

MINDFUL ACTIVITY:

Visualize yourself confidently facing a current challenge, feeling empowered by your strength.

DAY 356
RESILIENCE AND PERSEVERANCE

AFFIRMATION:

"I am capable of achieving my dreams
through resilience and dedication."

MINDFUL ACTIVITY:

Write down one dream and identify two steps
you can take to bring it closer to reality.

DAY 357
Mindfulness and Presence

Affirmation

"I embrace the present moment
with gratitude and awareness."

Mindful Activity:

Spend a few minutes observing your surroundings,
feeling gratitude for each detail in the present.

DAY 358

MANIFESTATION AND ABUNDANCE

AFFIRMATION:

"I am worthy of the abundance and joy I desire."

MINDFUL ACTIVITY:

Write down three things you desire, visualizing each one manifesting with gratitude.

DAY 359
FORGIVENESS AND LETTING GO

AFFIRMATION

"I let go of the past and open
myself to peace and joy."

MINDFUL ACTIVITY:

Reflect on one past hurt you're ready to release,
visualizing it dissolving with each breath.

DAY 360
Health and Wellness

Affirmation:

"I respect my body and treat it with love and care."

Mindful Activity:

Choose one small act of self-care today, such
as hydrating, stretching, or enjoying
a nourishing meal.

DAY 361
SELF-LOVE AND ACCEPTANCE

AFFIRMATION

"I am worthy of love and embrace myself fully."

MINDFUL ACTIVITY:

Reflect on one thing you appreciate about yourself today, taking a moment to honor it with self-compassion.

DAY 362
CONFIDENCE AND INNER STRENGTH

AFFIRMATION:

"I trust my journey and believe in my abilities."

MINDFUL ACTIVITY:

Visualize yourself achieving a personal goal, feeling the pride and confidence it brings you.

DAY 363
PEACE AND CALM

AFFIRMATION

"I choose peace and let go of what I cannot control."

MINDFUL ACTIVITY:

Close your eyes, breathe deeply, and imagine releasing any worries or tensions with each exhale.

DAY 364
Healing and Self-Compassion

Affirmation:

"I am patient with myself and honor
my healing journey."

Mindful Activity:

Place your hand on your heart, breathe deeply,
and acknowledge the progress you've
made with self-compassion.

DAY 365
SPIRITUALITY AND CONNECTION

AFFIRMATION

"I am grateful for my journey
and trust in the path ahead."

MINDFUL ACTIVITY:

Reflect on your journey over the past year, feeling
gratitude for every lesson and step forward.

EPILOGUE

As you reach the final pages of *365 Days of Affirmations*, take a moment to acknowledge the journey you've traveled. Each affirmation, each mindful moment, and each quiet reflection has contributed to the beautiful tapestry of growth, healing, and self-awareness you now carry forward.

Through the highs and lows, the grounding and uplifting, you've developed a practice of connecting with your inner strength and embracing the power of mindful intention. These affirmations may have helped you shift perspectives, unlock new layers of self-acceptance, or find peace and purpose in ways you didn't expect.

But know that this journey doesn't end here. These words are always available to you, ready to support you in times of need, guide you through moments of doubt, or inspire you to dream even bigger. Let the seeds planted here continue to grow in your heart and mind, becoming an integral part of your life's journey.

Remember, the true power of these affirmations lies in your commitment to nurturing the love, strength, and peace within yourself. As you step forward, may each day bring you closer to a life filled with harmony, purpose, and joy.

With gratitude for your journey,

Axel Jordan

ABOUT THE AUTHOR

Axel Jordan is a visionary author, Certified CBT & REBT Coach Practitioner, and Master Certified Sound Healer who has dedicated his life to inspiring mindfulness, personal growth, and holistic well-being. With over a decade of experience in sound therapy, coaching, and spiritual practices, Axel brings a unique blend of expertise and compassion to his work, empowering individuals to connect with their inner strength and embrace life with intention.

Raised in the vibrant cultural tapestry of Brooklyn, NYC, Axel's creativity and ability to connect deeply with others were shaped by his diverse upbringing. In *365 Days of Affirmations*, he channels his own journey of self-discovery, blending mindfulness, spirituality, and transformative practices to create a guide that uplifts and empowers readers each day.

Axel's career is as multifaceted as his writing, spanning music, healing, and cognitive coaching. His work reflects a deep understanding of the human experience, offering practical yet heartfelt tools for self-reflection and empowerment. Drawing from his expertise in sound healing and mindfulness, Axel infuses every affirmation with the wisdom to inspire transformation, inner peace, and resilience.

At home, Axel finds balance and joy in the company of his partner and the animals they foster together, embodying the compassion and grounding energy he encourages in his work.

When he's not writing or leading transformative sound bath sessions, Axel works closely with clients, guiding them on their journey to self-awareness, confidence, and fulfillment.

Axel's mission is to remind readers that growth is a daily practice and that small, mindful steps lead to profound change. With *365 Days of Affirmations*, he invites you to create a life of purpose, harmony, and gratitude— one day at a time.

365 Days Of Affirmations

thank you
&
happy healing
— axel

365 Days Of Affirmations

365 Day's Of Affirmations Copyright © 2024 by Axel Jordan.

All rights reserved. Printed in the United States of America. No part of this book may be used or reproduced in any manner whatsoever without written permission except in the case of reprints in the context of reviews.

www.AxelJordanBooks.com

Cover Design: Axel Jordan

ISBN: 979-8-89587-681-7

Library of Congress Control Number: 2024924254

ATTENTION: SCHOOL AND BUSINESSES

Any published works of Axel Jordan are available at quantity discounts with bulk purchase for educational, business, or sales promotional use.

For information, please contact:

www.AxelJordanBooks.com

www.ingramcontent.com/pod-product-compliance
Lightning Source LLC
Chambersburg PA
CBHW020918140626
46545CB00015B/99